Slow Cooker Cookbook

70 Kid-Friendly Slow Cooker Recipes- Family Cooking Series

@ www.kids-cooking-activities.com

Cooking in the slow cooker is something that brings forth a number of wonderful benefits. The foods taste better, is easier to prepare and cuts down on the time it takes to prepare dinner each day.

But, what do you do when you have kids that you want to prepare a meal for? It is often hard to make a meal because the children do not like what you are preparing or the ingredients are not healthy. Some parents would say this is even more true when trying to cook healthier and in a slow cooker. That is no longer the case.

In this cookbook, you will learn how to cook in the slow cooker like a pro preparing some of the tastiest meals that your family will love. Each of the meals in this slow cooker book are kid friendly and easy to prepare. Rest assured that you and your family are getting the most delicious and the healthiest meals that can be prepared all while giving you a bit of a break in the kitchen. These recipes are all kid tested and mom and dad approved so the whole family will enjoy eating them.

When you are ready to cook meals for the family in a whole new way this is the cookbook for you. Continue reading to experience some of the best kid-friendly slow cooker recipes that you can make.

Contents

The Benefits of Slow Cooking

To prepare a healthy and satisfying meal for the family it could take hours on end in the kitchen preparing a dinner. Although this may be perfectly suitable some nights, others are not so appealing for such great time lengths in the kitchen. What do you do when you want to feed the family a nutritious healthy and complete meal? You turn to the slow cooker.

Slow cooker meals taste great. The hours they're left in the pot to simmer lock in the flavors, the aroma, leaving only a delicious meal that your family will love. But wait, I have children you say; they would never eat anything coming from a slow cooker. You just need to understand the right kind of meals to prepare in the slow cooker to get the kids interesting.

Don't think that we've forgotten health in these recipes. It is hard enough to get kids to eat right without adding all of the extras that they don't need. Each recipe inside of this cookbook is made with natural and satisfying ingredients so they provide all of the nutrients, vitamins and minerals that you and your family need to stay strong and healthy.

On top of all of these fascinating facts, cooking with a slow cooker offers numerous benefits in itself. There are many reasons that people choose to reach for the slow cooker when it is time to cook, and it is not only dinner that you can use the cooker to make a meal. You can prepare a number of different recipes for all meals in your slow cooker, and when you do, here are some of the wonderful benefits that you can expect to come your way.

Benefits of Cooking with a Crock Pot

Slow cookers, or crock pots, depending on what you prefer to call them, offer the cook a number of exciting benefits that do not come with the use of a saucepan on the stove to cook. It is not often that a cook can get into the kitchen and make a fantastic meal that doesn't require a lot of time to be spent inside of the kitchen preparing that dish. Let's take a look at some of those great benefits that come your way with the use of the slow cooker. When you start preparing meals using the slow cooker all of these wonderful benefits can be yours, too, and these are just a handful of the many things that you can expect to find when you do.

Save Time

When a meal is prepared on top of the stove or in the oven you must be there to watch it, to stir and cook it. Otherwise it will burn, it won't cook evenly, etc. Not the case with the slow cooker. Once all of your steps for preparation have been completed you can put the meal in the crock pot, adjust the temperature and go about your life, all with the assurance that a great meal will be waiting for you in a few hours. You can really get more done cooking in a slow cooker, and you save a lot of dishes, too.

Use Cheaper Meats

When selecting meats to prepare for your family it is always important to pay special attention to the cut of meat chosen. Luckily with a slow cooker the cut of meat chosen is far less important, and you can take your pick of many different cuts that ordinarily couldn't be used. This saves a whole lot of money!

Use Less Energy

It takes far less energy to use a slow cooker than what is required to operate the stove, so there is even more money that can be saved and enjoyed. If you are looking for a way to eliminate some of the bills that you have this could be one of the best ways to do it. Using the cooker just one or two times per week could make a major difference here. Imagine what you can do with all of the money that is saved.

Healthier Foods

Cooking in the slow cooker is far healthier than cooking in the traditional methods. You eliminate all of the fat when using the slow cooker. All of the flavor of the meal is also locked into place during cooking.

Better Flavor

Cooking foods for the extended time which comes along with the slow cooker enables more of the food's natural flavors to come alive, and those are flavors that you will taste in every single bite. There is something very unique about the flavor of a meal when it is prepared in a slow cooker, and it is a taste that you won't find when you cook just anywhere. The exciting flavors that come alive are just one of the many reasons that so many people love to use the slow cooker to prepare all of their favorite meals and those soon to be favorites as well.

These are just some of the many exciting benefits that come to people who cook with a crock pot or a slow cooker. There isn't a question that you will enjoy the many rewards offered with slow cooker cooking on a regular basis.

That is the entire purpose of this guide. We're here to make life easy for you. Like you we have kids, and we also have busy lives.

The Recipes that you Want

Inside you will find mouthwatering, delicious and easy to make slow cooker meals the kids will love. All that you need is a crockpot and a few ingredients and you are on your way to an effortless and delicious meal. All of the recipes are kid tested and approved so there should be no problem getting your little one to eat up.

Breakfast, lunch, dinner and dessert, take a look at some of the best recipes that you can make in your slow cooker.

Slow Cooker Pasta Meals

There's no doubt that children love pasta, and they'll certainly love all of these easy slow cooker recipes. Try them all out with your family to score major brownie points while also preparing a fresh and healthy meal.

Cheesy Turkey & Sausage Spaghetti

Makes 4 servings

Ingredients

- 1 lb. Ground Turkey
- 1 lb. Ground Turkey Sausage
- 1 T.. Fresh Basil
- 1/4 tsp. Garlic Powder
- 1 tsp. Dried Sage
- 2 tsp. Marjoram
- 1/2 tsp. Ground Black Pepper
- 1/3 tsp. Ground Cayenne Pepper
- 1 Jar Spaghetti Sauce
- 1 tsp. Kosher Salt
- 1 Cup Ricotta Cheese
- 1 Cup Mozzarella Cheese, shredded
- 1 Cup Cottage Cheese
- 8 oz. Whole Wheat Spaghetti

Directions

1. Combine the oregano, dried sage, cayenne pepper, ground turkey, garlic powder and ground black pepper in a large bowl.
2. In a skillet on medium heat, cook the turkey sausage until no longer pink and brown on the

outside, or about 12 minutes. Break into small pieces.

3. Drain grease from the sausage and add spaghetti noodles, uncooked, as well as the marina.
4. In another bowl, combine the turkey sausage mixture with the remaining ingredients.
5. Place inside of slow cooker and cook on low for 3 hours.

Creamy Chicken & Broccoli Spaghetti

Makes 4 servings.

Ingredients

- 2 lb. chicken breasts
- 1 tsp Oregano
- 4 Cups homemade pasta sauce
- 1/8 tsp salt
- Pinch fresh ground black pepper
- 1 box spaghetti noodles
- 1/2 Cup Ricotta cheese
- 5 Cups fresh Broccoli

Directions

1. Put the spaghetti sauce in the slow cooker and add cut up pieces of chicken breast. Add salt, pepper and the oregano. Coat the chicken in the sauce; cook for 6 hours.
2. Prepare spaghetti according to directions. Five minutes before pastas is al dente, add broccoli.
3. Drain the spaghetti. Shred the chicken into the crockpot and add the noodles.

4. Add Ricotta cheese.

5. Serve.

Slow-Cooker Lasagna

Makes one lasagna, serves 4 to 6

Ingredients

- 5-6 tomatoes, chopped
- 1 Tablespoon dried Oregano
- 3 Cloves chopped Garlic
- Kosher Salt
- Fresh Ground Black Pepper
- 1 lb. Ricotta cheese
- 1 T. dried Parsley
- 12 ounce package lasagna noodles
- 1/2 Cup grated Parmesan cheese
- 1 1/2 Cups Mozzarella cheese, shredded

Directions

1. Combine the tomatoes, oregano, pinch of salt, 1/2 teaspoon pepper and garlic in a bowl.
2. In a second bowl, combine dash pepper, ricotta, parsley and the Parmesan.
3. Add 1/3 of the tomatoes to a six quart slow cooker. Add a layer of broken noodles. Top with 1/3 of the Ricotta mixture and another 1/3 of the tomato mixture.
4. Sprinkle with 1/3 of the ricotta. Add noodles and repeat process until all ingredients are used.
5. Cover and cook on low for 3 to 4 hours.

Spaghetti with Meatballs

Ingredients

- 1 pound ground beef, chicken or turkey
- 2 T. dried onion
- 1 tsp garlic powder
- 2 egg whites
- 12 ounces spaghetti
- large jar, 26 oz, spaghetti sauce
- 1/2 cup shredded Mozzarella cheese

Directions

1. Combine together ground meat, onion, garlic and egg whites.
2. Form into balls.
3. Add large jar of spaghetti sauce
4. Add to the slow cooker.
5. Cook on high for 5 to 6 hours.
6. When done, prepare pasta according to package directions
7. Add cheese to top meatballs and allow to melt while pasta is cooking.
8. Serve pasta topped with meatball sauce.

Pizza Pasta

Makes 1 pizza

Ingredients

- 8 lasagna noodles, broken in pieces
- 1/2 Cup cooked ground beef
- 12 pepperoni slices
- 12 Canadian bacon slices
- 1/4 T. garlic
- 1/2 T. oregano
- 2 Cups mozzarella cheese
- 1 Cup spaghetti or pizza sauce
- 1/2 Cup water

Directions

1. Add half of the sauce to the bottom of the slow cooker.
2. Sprinkle 1/3 cheese, the pizza toppings* and spices to the top of the sauce.
3. Add broken lasagna noodles and repeat the layers.
4. Cook in the slow cooker for 4 to 6 hours, on low.

*Add in mushrooms, olives, peppers or other pizza toppings you'd like.

Chicken Primavera

Makes 6 servings.

Ingredients

- 3 Cups spaghetti or marinara sauce
- 12 Oz. Boneless, skinless chicken breasts
- 2 Cups cooked fresh spinach
- 2 Cups fresh cooked broccoli florets
- 1 Cup zucchini, sliced
- 6 oz. Penne Pasta
- 1/2 Cup Parmesan

Directions

1. Combine all of the ingredients in the slow cooker.
2. Cover with lid.
3. Cook for 6 to 8 hours on low setting.

~Add or replace any of the vegetables for ones your kids like.

Baked Ziti

Makes 8 servings

Ingredients

- 1 lb. box of ziti noodles, uncooked
- 2 egg whites
- 1/2 Cup Parmesan cheese + ½ cup
- 15 ounce container low-fat ricotta cheese
- pinch of salt
- 1/2 Cup + 1 Cup mozzarella cheese
- 1/2 tsp salt
- 6 Cups homemade spaghetti sauce
- dash pepper
- 1 tsp dried basil

Directions

1. Use olive oil to coat a 6-quart slow cooker.
2. In a bowl, combine 1/2 Cup Parmesan, 1/2 Cup Mozzarella, and egg whites. Season with salt and pepper.
3. Add 1/2 of the noodles in the slow cooker.
4. Pour 2 cups pasta sauce over the pasta.
5. Add two to three spoonful's of the cheese mixture.
6. Repeat the steps starting with the noodles.
7. Cook for 4 to 6 hours on low.
8. When finished, sprinkle mozzarella cheese and Parmesan over the top and cook another 20 minutes.
9. Add basil for garnish.

~If you'd like to add meat to this dish, ground beef and stir into spaghetti sauce.

Slow Cooker Italian Style Penne

Makes 6 servings

Ingredients
- 1 Cup diced tomatoes
- 1 Cup kidney beans
- 1 zucchini, cut in small pieces
- 1 tsp. Italian herb seasoning
- 8 oz. whole wheat penne pasta
- 1 tsp. garlic powder
- 1/2 Cup low sodium, chicken broth
- 1 tsp. onion powder
- Balsamic Vinegar to taste
- Parmesan cheese, topping

Directions
1. Spray inside of crock pot with cooking spray.
2. Add the pasta in a single layer to the bottom of the slow cooker. Pour tomatoes on top, followed by the beans and zucchini. Add 2 cups water to the mixture.
3. Add onion, garlic, Italian herbs and cover with lid.
4. Cook on low for 2 hours.
5. Add 2 teaspoons Balsamic vinegar before serving, if desired.
6. Top with a sprinkle of Parmesan.

Crockpot Macaroni and Cheese

Makes 4-6 servings

Ingredients

3 Cups macaroni noodles
3 Cups shredded cheese, combination of favorites
flavors or cheddar cheese
2 Cups evaporated milk
2 T. butter
salt and pepper to taste
dash hot pepper

Directions

Spray inside of slow cooker with cooking spray or rub
with oil. Combine all the ingredients together inside of
slow cooker. Cook on low and for 4 to 5 hours, stirring
several times during cooking.

Spaghetti Squash
Makes 4-6 servings

Ingredients

1 lb ground beef, browned
14 oz or 1 3/4 Cups chicken broth
1 can (6 oz size) tomato paste
1 1/2 tsp Italian seasoning
1 tsp garlic powder
1 tsp onion powder
dash salt and black pepper
1 medium spaghetti squash
Parmesan cheese for topping

Directions
Brown beef and drain off extra grease. Add to crock pot and top with remaining ingredients except the spaghetti squash.
Cut squash in half lengthwise and scoop out seeds. Place spaghetti squash halves into the meat sauce cut side down.
Cook in slow cooker on low for 4 hours or until the spaghetti squash is fork tender.
Take out squash and with a fork pull out strands of the squash.
To serve, add "Spaghetti" squash into each bowl and top with sauce. Sprinkle with Parmesan cheese..

Slow Cooker Chicken Recipes

These slow cooker chicken recipes are sure to be a hit with kids of all ages, and mom and dad, too. Chicken is healthy, full of flavor and so versatile it can be prepared over and over again in a new and exciting method.

Moroccan Lemon Chicken

Makes 8 servings

Ingredients

- 12 boneless, skinless chicken breasts
- 1 tsp pepper, divided
- pinch salt, to taste
- 1 sliced lemon
- 2 T. Olive oil, divided
- 2 T. Lemon Juice
- 1Cup flour
- 1/2 tsp Ground Cumin
- 1 Cup green olives

Directions

1. Season chicken breasts with a pinch of salt and pepper.
2. Add chicken to the slow cooker top with lemon slices.
3. In a bowl. blend together cumin, flour and lemon juice. Pour over chicken.
4. Top with olives.
5. Cook for 6 to 8 hours on low heat.

Seasoned Roast Chicken

Makes 6 servings.

Ingredients

- 1 large roasting chicken
- 2 minced garlic cloves
- 3 tsp olive oil
- 11/4 tsp black pepper
- 11/4 tsp paprika
- 2 1/2 tsp fresh thyme
- Kosher salt to taste
- 2 stalks celery
- 1/2 Cup water
- 2 Cup carrots, chopped
- 2 potatoes, chopped

Directions

1. Coat the chicken with olive oil.
2. In a bowl, blend together garlic, pepper, paprika, thyme and salt. Rub on the chicken.
3. Add 1/2 Cup water to the crockpot and add celery stalks cut in pieces.
4. Place the chicken in the crock pot.
5. Add the chopped potatoes and carrots.
6. Cover with a lid and cook on high for about 4 hours, or until chicken is done.

Fried Chicken

Makes 6 servings

Ingredients:

- 3 chicken breasts
- 1/2 Cup Buttermilk
- 1 Cup Bread Crumbs
- 1 egg white
- 1/2 tsp black pepper
- 1/2 tsp cumin
- pinch salt to taste
- 1/2 tsp. garlic powder

Directions:

1. Spray cooker with olive oil or cooking spray.
2. In a bowl, combine the egg and buttermilk.
3. In a separate bowl, combine the flour and spices.
4. In a another dish, add the bread crumbs.
5. Dip each chicken breast into the egg mixture, and then into the flour mixture.
6. Dip the chicken breasts in the egg a second time, and follow it the bread crumbs. Repeat for each chicken breast.
7. Put each piece of chicken in the slow cooker. Add pepper to taste.
8. Cover with lid and cook for 3 hours on high.

Slow Cooker Pomegranate Chicken

Yields 4

Ingredients

- 4 boneless, skinless chicken breasts
- 1/2 tsp salt
- 1/2 tsp black pepper
- 1 tsp chili powder
- 1 tsp dried oregano
- 1 tsp coriander
- 2 cloves minced garlic
- 2 Cups pomegranate juice (use sugar free)
- 2 T. extra virgin olive oil
- 2 T. honey
- 1 T. Dijon mustard
- 1 T. white balsamic vinegar

Directions

1. Combine herbs and spices together in a bowl.
2. Add the olive oil and the herbs and spices and mix well.
3. Coat each breast of chicken with the herb and oil mixture.
4. Add to the slow cooker.
5. In a bowl, combine the juice and vinegar with the garlic, honey and the mustard.
6. Pour mixture over the chicken.
7. Cook on high for 6 to 7 hours.

Chicken Fajitas

Makes 6

Ingredients

- 2 lbs. boneless, skinless chicken breasts
- 1 Cup of freshly prepared salsa
- 1/2 T. dried oregano
- 1 T. chili powder
- 1 T. ground cumin
- 1 white onion, sliced and peeled
- 1/2 tsp salt
- tortilla shells
- Sour Cream, topping

Directions

1. In a bowl, combine all ingredients except the chicken breasts. Mix well.
2. Coat each of the chicken breasts in the mixture.
3. Pour into a crockpot.
4. Cook on high heat for 4 hours.
5. Shred meat into bite size pieces.
6. Warm tortillas in microwave.
7. Top each tortilla with filling.
8. Add sour cream if desired.

Barbeque Chicken Melts

Yields 5 servings.

Ingredients

- 5 chicken breasts
- 2 Cups bottled or homemade barbeque sauce
- English muffins
- 1/2 Cup Cheddar Cheese

Directions

1. Put the chicken breasts in the slow cooker. Top with barbeque sauce. Stir until well coated. Cook for 6-8 hours on low.
2. Pull chicken apart using a fork.
3. Warm English muffins in oven or toaster.
4. Top each of the muffins with chicken and sprinkle with cheese.
5. Place bake in oven for an additional 3 to 4 minutes, or until cheese is melted.

Chicken Chili

Makes 8 servings.

Ingredients

- 2-3 Cups rotisserie chicken or shredded chicken
- 1 Cup sweet onion, diced finely
- 2 garlic cloves, minced
- 1 can chopped tomatoes or 4 fresh tomatoes chopped
- 1 Cup tomato paste
- 2 Cups water
- 2 T. chili powder or less, according to your taste
- 1/2 tsp ground black pepper
- pinch of salt, to taste
- 1 Cup Navy beans
- 1 Cup Kidney beans
- 1/2 Cup Cheddar Cheese

Directions

1. Mix all of the ingredients together in a slow cooker.
2. Cook on low in the slow cooker for 4 to 6 hours.
3. Sprinkle each serving with cheddar cheese, if desired.

Chicken Potatoes & Carrots

Makes 4 servings

Ingredients

- 6 chicken thighs
- 4 potatoes, small
- 1 onion, chopped
- 2 Cups carrots
- 1 tsp minced garlic
- 1/2 tsp pepper
- 1 1/2 tsp salt
- 1 tsp paprika

Directions

1. Add onions to the slow cooker.
2. Cut potatoes into cubes and add to the cooker.
3. Add potatoes and carrots to the top.
4. Add salt and pepper as well as the garlic and paprika.
5. Place chicken on top of the mixture.
6. Cook in the slow cooker on low for 6 to 8 hours.

Slow Cooker Pulled Chicken Sandwiches

Ingredients

- 2 lbs. chicken breast halves
- 2 Onions, sliced
- 1 tsp canola oil
- 2 T. cider vinegar
- 1 Cup ketchup
- 1/2 tsp garlic powder
- 1/2 tsp ground cumin
- 1 tsp onion powder
- 2 T. molasses
- 1 T. Dijon mustard

Directions

1. Put onion in a 6-quart slow cooker.
2. Heat a skillet on medium heat on the stove.
3. Put the chicken in the slow cooker.
4. Combine the ketchup along with the 6 ingredients and pour on top of the chicken.
5. Cook the mixture on low for 4 to 6 hours.
6. Mixture should be thick.
7. Remove the chicken from the cooker and use a fork to shred it.
8. Stir shredded meat with the sauce until well covered.
9. Top a bun with shredded chicken and serve.

Chicken Parmesan

Serves 4

Ingredients

- 4 boneless, skinless chicken breast halves
- 1/2 Cup Parmesan cheese
- 1/2 Cup bread crumbs
- 1T. Italian seasoning
- pinch of salt and pepper
- 6 slices Mozzarella cheese
- 1 Cup homemade marina sauce
- 1 egg, well beaten
- 12 ounces fettuccine noodles

Directions

1. Rub inside of slow cooker with oil or cooking spray.
2. In a bowl, mix the egg.
3. In another bowl, combine the cheese, bread crumbs and spices.
4. Dip each breast of chicken into the egg and toss into the bread crumb mixture and coat well.
5. Place the chicken in the crockpot.
6. Top each chicken with a slice of the Mozzarella.
7. Cover with the marina.
8. Cook on low, covered, for 8 hours.
9. Prepare fettuccini according to package directions.
10. Add chicken breasts to pasta and serve.

Slow Cooker Soup Recipes

Chicken Noodle Soup

Makes 8 servings.

Ingredients

- 2 lbs. chicken breast
- 1 lb. Baby Carrots
- 1/2 tsp dried thyme
- 1 tsp salt
- 1 T. chopped onion
- 1 Garlic clove, minced
- 1/4 tsp pepper
- 2 stalks celery, chopped
- 4 Cups water
- 1 Cup Pea Pods
- 3 Cups uncooked Egg Noodles

Directions

1. Combine the chicken, onion, garlic, water, thyme, salt and pepper and the celery in a 4 quart cooker.
2. Cover with lid.
3. On a low temperature, cook for 6 to 8 hours.
4. Add the noodles and the pea pods and turn to high.
5. Return lid to the pot and cook for an additional half hour.
6. Remove chicken from the slow cooker and cut into small chunks. Add back to soup.

Smoky Pea Soup

Yields 6 servings.

Ingredients

- 2 Ham Hocks
- 2 chopped carrots
- 2 chopped celery stalks
- 1/2 lb. Split peas
- 1 tsp dried thyme
- 2 cloves chopped garlic
- 1 onion, chopped
- 2 Cups water
- pinch of salt and pepper

Directions

1. Put the ham hocks in a 6-quart slow cooker.
2. Add the onion, garlic, thyme, celery, peas and the carrots along with the water.
3. Cover with a lid.
4. Cook until the meat is done, or for about 6-8 hours, on low.
5. Put the ham hocks in a plate; shred meat from the bones.
6. Return the ham to the soup and serve.

Cauliflower Bacon Chowder

Makes 4 servings.

Ingredients
3 slices bacon, cut up small and fried crisp
1 bag (16 oz) frozen cauliflower, thawed
1/4 Cup diced onion
1 garlic clove, minced
1/2 T. dried parsley
1 tsp kosher salt
1/4 tsp black pepper
1/4 tsp dried thyme
28 oz. chicken broth
1-2 Cups heavy cream

Directions
Add all ingredients except cream to slow cooker.
Cook on low for 4-6 hours.
Before serving stir in cream.

White Bean Chili

Makes 8 servings.

Ingredients
- 3 uncooked chicken breasts, cut into small pieces
- 1/2 Cup sweet onion, chopped
- 2 cloves minced garlic
- 1 Cup diced tomatoes
- 2 T. tomato paste
- 2 Cups water
- pinch of salt and pepper
- 2 cans drained Cannelloni beans
- 2 tsp chili powder, according to taste
- small can or 1 1/2 Cup sweet corn

Directions
1. Add all ingredients to a slow cooker.
2. Cover the pot and cook on high for 6 to 7 hours.

Vegetable Soup

Makes 8 servings

Ingredients
1 potato, diced
1 sweet onion, chopped
1 Cup fresh whole-kernel corn
1 Cup fresh green beans, broken into pieces
4 carrots, sliced
pinch of salt and pepper
1/2 tsp paprika
3 Cups V8 or tomato juice
2 Cups water

Directions
1.   Add all of the ingredients to a 6-quart slow cooker.
2.   Cover with lid.
3.   Cook on low for 6-8 hours.

Beef Stew

Serves 6

Ingredients

- 1 lb. Round Steak, chopped
- pinch of salt and pepper, to taste
- 1 white onion, chopped
- 2 Cups potatoes, chopped
- 1 T. thyme
- 2 carrots, chopped
- 3 garlic cloves, minced
- 4 celery sticks, chopped
- 2 Cups water
- 2 Cups beef broth
- 1 Cup diced tomatoes
- 1 T. Worcestershire sauce

Directions

1. Add diced potatoes, onions, celery and carrots to slow cooker.
2. Season meat with salt and pepper and place on top of vegetables.
3. Pour broth, tomatoes and water over all.
4. Cover with the lid and cook for 6-8 hours.

Easy Coleslaw Vegetable Soup
Serves 4-6

Ingredients
2 bags (14 oz size) coleslaw (or 1 head cabbage shredded)
1 onion, diced
2 celery stalks, diced
1 green bell pepper, diced
1 carrot, diced
1 can (14 oz) diced tomatoes
1 can (8 oz) tomato sauce
2 garlic cloves, grated
26 oz beef or vegetable broth
2 Cups water
1/2 package dry onion soup mix, or according to your tastes

Directions
Add all ingredients into the slow cooker and stir together. Cook on low for 6-8 hours or until cabbage is tender.

Cream Of Broccoli Cheese Soup

Serves 4-6

Ingredients

2 heads of broccoli, chopped
1 large onion, diced
2 celery stalks, diced
48 oz or 6 Cups chicken broth
1/2 tsp cumin
1/2 tsp Worcestershire sauce
1 Cup heavy cream
2 Cups shredded mild Cheddar or American cheese
kosher salt and black pepper to taste

Directions

1. Add broccoli, onion, celery and chicken broth into slow cooker.
2. Cook on low for 6-8 hours.
3. Blend soup with an immersion blender or puree in blender.
4. Add back to slow cooker and stir in cumin, Worcestershire sauce, cream and cheese.
5. Stir until well combined and heat until cheese is melted.

Easy Taco Chili

Serves 4-6
Ingredients
16 oz. kidney beans
2 T. or more to taste, taco seasoning mix
32 oz. can tomatoes or 4-5 fresh tomatoes, chopped
1 lb. Ground beef browned
1 onion, chopped
1 1/2 Cups water

Directions

1. Brown beef and onion together. Drain off excess grease.
2. Mix all ingredients together into slow cooker and cook for 4-5 hours on low.

Serve with any of these toppings
small avocado, diced
cheddar cheese, shredded
sour cream
tortilla chips

Penne Vegetable Soup
Serves 4-6

Ingredients
28 oz or 4 Cups beef broth
1 can (14 oz) diced tomatoes
1 pkg (16 oz) frozen mixed vegetables
2 Cups water
1/2 tsp garlic salt
1/8 tsp black pepper
1 1/2 Cups penne noodles, uncooked

Directions

1. Add all ingredients except noodles to slow cooker.
2. Cook on low for 6 hours.
3. Add pasta 30 minutes before ready to serve.

Slow Cooker Seafood Recipes

You can cook seafood in a slow cooker as well. However most recipes will not take more than a few hours to cook so keep this in mind when planning.

Jambalaya

Makes 8 servings

Ingredients

- 2 lbs. skinless, boneless chicken, cut
- 1 Cup diced tomatoes
- 1 onion, chopped
- 2 Cups celery, chopped
- 2 tsp dried oregano
- 1 green bell pepper, chopped
- 1 lb. smoked sausage
- 1 Cup Water
- 1 tsp Cayenne Pepper
- 1 lb. Cooked Shrimp

Directions

1. Mix all of the ingredients together in a slow cooker, expect for the shrimp.
2. Cook for 8 hours on low.
3. Add the shrimp 45 minutes before the mixture is ready.

Lemon Dijon Salmon

Makes 6

Ingredients

- 2 chicken bouillon cubes
- 1/2 Cup chopped onion
- 2 tsp olive oil
- 2 tsp minced garlic
- 2 lbs. Salmon Fillet patties
- 1 Cup Barley
- 1 tsp dried dill weed
- Salt
- Pepper

For Sauce

- 1/4 Cup Dijon mustard
- 3 T. olive oil
- 3 T. lemon juice
- 1 tsp minced garlic
- 1/2 Cup sour cream

Directions:

1. Combine olive oil, onion and garlic in a bowl and microwave for 6 minutes.
2. Place mixture in the slow cooker.
3. Add dill weed and bouillon, barley and water to the pot. Stir well.
4. Add a pinch of salt and pepper to the salmon.
5. Place salmon filets on top of slow cooker mixture in a single layer.
6. Cook on high for 1 1/2 hours.
7. Combine all of the ingredients for the sauce together in a bowl.

8. When salmon is ready, pour the lemon
   Dijon sauce on top.

Seafood Stew
Makes 8 servings

Ingredients

- 1 bottle clam juice
- 2 Cups chopped onion
- 1 Cup water
- 1 can tomato paste
- 2 cloves garlic, minced
- 1Cup tomatoes
- 1/4 tsp sugar
- 1 T. red wine vinegar
- 3 T. Italian seasoning
- 1 T. olive oil
- 1 lb. White Fish, cut into pieces
- 1 lb. Uncooked shrimp (remove tails)
- 1/3 cup fresh parsley
- 1 can crabmeat

Directions

1. Use a 6-quart slow cooker.
2. Combine clam juice, tomato paste, oil, vinegar, sugar, Italian seasoning and the garlic and tomatoes in the cooker.
3. Cook on high for 4 hours.
4. Add the clams, crabmeat and shrimp to the slow cooker.
5. Reduce to a low heat setting.
6. Cover the slow cooker.
7. Simmer for an additional one hour.
8. Top with parsley.

Maple Salmon

Makes 6 servings

Ingredients

- 6 salmon fillets
- 1/2 Cup maple syrup
- 1/2 Cup soy sauce
- 1/8 Cup(s) lime juice
- 1 tsp fresh ginger, minced
- 2 tsp crushed garlic

Directions

1. Put salmon in a 4- quart crock pot.
2. In a bowl, mix remaining ingredients together.
3. Pour mixture on top of the salmon in the crock pot.
4. Cover with lid.
5. Cook on high for 1 hour.

Feta Shrimp & Chicken

8 servings

Ingredients

- 4 chicken breasts
- 3 cloves garlic, minced
- 1 onion, chopped
- 1 tsp. salt
- 4 T. lemon juice
- 1/2 Cup water
- 8 oz. Shrimp, cooked and drained
- 1/2 Cup Feta cheese, crumbled
- 1 Cup Penne Pasta, cooked

Directions

1. Put onion and garlic in the crock pot.
2. Top with chicken.
3. Add tomatoes, water, salt and lemon juice.
4. Cover with lid.
5. Cook for 6 to 8 hours on low heat.
6. When done, add to serving bowls and sprinkle with feta and cooked pasta.

Slow Cooker Vegetarian Recipes

It isn't always necessary to have meat to make a great meal. How about a few delicious vegetarian slow cooker recipes? You can feel great about serving any of these great choices to your family.

Vegetarian Fajitas

Makes 8 Fajitas

Ingredients

- 4 ounces diced green chilies
- 1 green bell pepper, seeds removed and sliced
- 1 red bell pepper, seeds removed and sliced
- 3 diced tomatoes
- 1 onion, diced
- 1/2 tsp garlic salt
- 1/2 tsp dried oregano
- 2 tsp cumin
- 1 teaspoons vegetable oil
- 1 teaspoons chili powder

Directions

1. Spray a 4-quart crock pot with nonstick cooking spray.
2. Combine all of the ingredients together in the slow cooker. Mix until well combined.
3. Cook for 6 to 7 hours on low.
4. Add vegetables to a tortilla and top with sour cream, if desired.

Vegetarian Chili
Makes 8 servings

Ingredients
- 1 can diced tomatoes
- 1 can black beans, drained
- 1 can cannellini beans, drained
- 1 can red kidney beans, drained
- 1 Cup onion, chopped
- 1 can corn kernels
- 2 Cups water
- 1 Cup lima beans
- 1 green bell pepper, seeded and chopped
- 1 T. chili powder
- 1 T. ground cumin
- 2 T. oregano
- 2 cloves garlic, minced
- 1/2 Cup couscous
- 1/2 Cup shredded cheese
- pinch of Salt and Pepper, to taste

Directions

1. Add all of the ingredients to the slow cooker, with the exception of the salt and pepper, shredded cheese and couscous.
2. Cover with lid.
3. Cook for 8 to 9 hours on low.
4. Add couscous 10 minutes before ready.
5. Top with shredded cheese and serve.

Bean & Barley Soup

Makes 8 servings

Ingredients

- 1 Cup Great Northern beans
- 3 cloves garlic minced
- 1/2 cup barley
- 2 carrots, chopped
- 1/2 onion, chopped
- pepper and salt, to taste
- 2 tablespoons Italian seasoning
- 1 can tomatoes
- 1/2 cup Balsamic Vinegar

Directions

1. Add 6 cups of water, carrots, onions, garlic and beans to the slow cooker. Season with pepper and salt.
2. Add tomatoes.
3. Cover and cook for 6-8 hours.
4. Season with salt and pepper if needed and drizzle each serving with Balsamic vinegar.

Spinach & Bean Enchiladas

Makes 4 servings

Ingredients

- 1 can black beans
- 1 Cup corn
- 1/2 teaspoon ground cumin
- 1 Cup spinach, cooked
- 8 ounces Cheddar Cheese
- 1 jar salsa
- Kosher salt
- Ground Black Pepper
- 8 corn tortilla shells
- 1 head lettuce chopped

Directions

1. Mash half of the beans in a bowl and mix in the cumin, 1 cup of cheddar cheese, corn and the spinach. Add salt, pepper and the rest of the beans.
2. Add 1jar of salsa to the crock pot. Roll the bean mixture into the tortillas and line in the slow cooker.
3. Top with cheese and remaining salsa.
4. Cook for 3 to 4 hours.
5. Top each serving with shredded lettuce and sour cream, if desired.

Squash Lasagna
Makes 6 servings

Ingredients

- 2 Cups chopped winter squash or pumpkin
- 14/ teaspoon Ground Nutmeg
- Ground Black Pepper
- dash salt
- 16 oz container Ricotta
- 6 Cups baby spinach
- 1 box lasagna noodles
- 1/8 tsp ground nutmeg
- Green Salad
- 1/2 Cups Mozzarella

Directions
1. In a bowl combine the nutmeg and the squash.
2. In another bowl combine spinach. Season with salt and pepper.
3. Add 1/2 cup of the squash mixture to the slow cooker.
4. Top with 3 broken lasagna noodles. Add another layer of squash and a layer of the ricotta cheese mixture.
5. Repeat until all of the ingredients are used.
6. Top with Mozzarella.
7. Cook for 3 to 4 hours on low.

Slow Cooker Pork Recipes

Apricot Sauce with Pork Chops

Ingredients

pork roast
apricot jam or 4-5 fresh apricots, chopped
1/3 Cup lemon juice
1/3 Cup ketchup
1/4 Cup chicken broth
3 T, honey
1 T. soy sauce
1/8 to 1/4 teaspoon ground ginger

Directions

1. Add pork roast to crock pot.
2. Stir together apricot, lemon juice, ketchup, broth, honey, soy sauce and ginger together until well combined.
3. Pour over pork roast.
4. Cook 8-10 hours on low.
5. Shred or slice pork and serve with apricot sauce.

Pork Tacos
Makes 6 servings

Ingredients

- 2 Cups salsa, plus extra for topping
- 1 T. chili powder
- 2 T . cocoa powder
- Kosher Salt
- 3 lbs. Boneless Pork roast
- 18 corn tortillas
- 1/2 Cup sour cream

Directions

1. Add the chili powder, cocoa, oregano, salsa and salt in a slow cooker. Add the pork and marinate well.
2. Cover with a lid and cook for 6-8 hours on low.
3. When pork is ready, use a fork to shred the meat
4. Warm tortillas in the microwave before serving
5. Serve inside of the tortilla shells with sour cream and extra salsa. You can also add shredded lettuce or guacamole.

Root Beer Pork Tenders
Serves 6 to 8

Ingredients
3 lbs pork roast, boneless
1/2 tsp kosher salt
1/2 tsp black pepper
1 T. cooking oil
2 small onions, sliced thin
2 cans (12 oz ea) diet root beer
4 garlic cloves, minced
1 can (8 oz) tomato sauce
1 tsp Tabasco sauce

Directions

1. Season pork with salt and pepper and brown on all sides in a hot skillet.
2. Add onions, root beer, garlic, tomato sauce and Tabasco sauce to slow cooker.
3. Add browned pork to top of ingredients.
4. Cook 6-8 hours on low.
5. Shred pork with a fork and serve.

Lemon & Sage Pork

Makes 6 servings

Ingredients

3 lbs pork roast
2 T. flour
pinch of salt and pepper to taste
2 T. olive oil
4 cloves garlic, minced
4 Cups whole milk
1 tsp grated lemon peel
5 fresh sage leaves

Directions

1. Season pork roast with salt and pepper. Roll in 2 T. flour.
2. In a skillet, add oil and heat.
3. Brown pork on each side and place in slow cooker.
4. In the same skillet, add the sage and the garlic. Cook for 1 minute or until brown.
5. Add to the slow cooker, with the lemon peel and the milk.
6. Cook in the slow cooker for 8 to 9 hours, or until meat is brown and tender.
7. Slice on a carving board.

Pork Caritas

Makes 6 servings

Ingredients

1 sliced onion
2 T. chipotles
3 lb. Pork Roast
4 cloves Garlic, minced
Salt
Pepper
1/2 Cup water
1 T. vegetable oil
1 pkg. Corn Tortillas

Directions

1. Combine the water, onion and chipotles in a slow cooker. Stir well.
2. Add salt and pepper to season.
3. Brown roast on each side.
4. Transfer to the slow cooker.
5. Add 1/2 Cup water.
6. Cover with a lid and cook on high for 6 to 7 hours.
7. When ready, use a fork to shred the pork and stir into juices in the crock pot.
8. Serve with tortillas.

Peachy Pork Chops

Serves 6

Ingredients

1/4 Cup brown sugar
can cream of mushroom soup
1 T. Worcestershire sauce
1/4 Cup water
1/2 tsp cinnamon
1/4 Cup peach juice from can peaches
2 Cups fresh peaches or canned peaches
6 boneless pork chops

Directions

1. Add pork chops to slow cooker.
2. Stir together sugar, cinnamon, soup, Worcestershire sauce, peach juice and water. Pour over pork chops.
3. Add peaches to top.
4. Cook 4-6 hours on high.

Apple Cherry Stuffed Pork Chops

Ingredients

- 1 Celery Stalk, chopped
- 1 Apple, peeled and chopped
- 1/2 loaf bread
- 1 T. dried basil
- 1 onion, diced
- 1/2 Cup butter
- 1 1/2 Cups Dried Cherries
- 1 Cup water
- 6 Pork Loin Chops

Directions

1. Combine all of the ingredients in a bowl, expect the pork loin. Add half of the mixture to the slow cooker.
2. When well combined, place pork on top of the mixture. Top with the remaining mixture.
3. Cover with lid.
4. Cook for 7 to 9 hours on low heat.

Vegetable Pork Stew

Makes 6 servings

Ingredients

- 2 lb. pork roast
- 1/2 Cup chopped onion
- 3 carrots, cut
- 2 Cups parsnips
- 2 Cups butternut squash
- 1 T. sage leaves
- 4 Cups water
- pinch of salt and pepper
- 4 T. butter, melted
- 3 T. all-purpose flour

Directions:

1. Cut pork into cubes and season with salt and pepper.
2. Place pork into a slow cooker with the remaining ingredients except for the flour and the melted butter.
3. Cover and cook for 7 to 8 hours on low.
4. In a bowl, mix the melted butter and the flour.
5. Add to the slow cooker and stir well.
6. Turn the slow cooker to high temperature.
7. Cover with the lid and cook an additional one hour.

Easy Pork Sandwiches
Makes 8 sandwiches.

Ingredients
- 16 hamburger buns
- 3 lbs. Boneless Pork Roast
- 1 1/2 tablespoon Sea Salt
- 2 tablespoons Liquid Smoke
- 1 boneless pork roast

Directions
1. Slit holes into the pork roast. Season with salt.
2. Place the pork into a 4 quart slow cooker. Add 1 tablespoon of liquid smoke to the pork.
3. Cover and cook on low for 10-12 hours.
4. When done, remove the pork roast from the slow cooker.
5. Put on a cutting board and slice the pork with a knife or a fork.
6. Place mixture into each of the buns and serve with your favorite sides.

Teriyaki Pork Roast

Ingredients

1/2 Cup soy sauce
2 Tablespoons Worcestershire sauce
1/2 Cup water
4 teaspoon ginger
2 garlic cloves, minced

pork roast

Directions

1. Blend ingredients together in a measuring cup until well combined.
2. In a slow cooker, add a 2-3 lb. pork roast.
3. Pour sauce over the top of pork and cook 6-8 hours on high.
4. Shred or slice meat and serve.

Slow Cooker Beef Recipes

Beef Black-Eyed Pea Stew

Ingredients

2 lbs. beef stew meat
1 bag (16 oz) dried black-eyed peas
1 can (10 oz) beef broth
5 carrots, chopped
4 Cups water
salt and pepper to taste
flour
oil

Directions

1. Sprinkle beef stew meat with flour and season with salt and pepper. Toss to coat.
2. Brown beef in a skillet.
3. Rinse black eyed peas and place in slow cooker.
4. Top with browned beef, broth, carrots and water.
5. Cook on low for 8-10 hours until black eyed peas are tender.

Macaroni & Beef

Ingredients

- 1 onion, diced or grated
- 2 lbs. ground beef
- 1 tsp Kosher Salt
- 8 ounce elbow macaroni
- Fresh Ground Black Pepper
- 2 T. fresh basil
- 1/2 Cup Parmesan

Directions

1. Add onion to the crock pot. Crumble the ground beef over the top. Add tomatoes to the top.
2. Cook for 4 to 6 hours on low heat.
3. Season with pepper and salt.
4. Cook pasta according to the directions on the package.
5. Top each bowl of noodles with meat sauce and Parmesan.
6. Add basil for garnish.

Beef Stroganoff

Makes 8 servings

Ingredients

- 3 T. olive oil
- 2 pounds beef top sirloin steak, cut
- 1 onion, chopped
- 1 Cup water
- 1 T. tomato paste
- 1 pound baby Portobello mushrooms
- 3 T. butter
- 1/2 Cup Beef Broth
- 2 tsp Ground Mustard
- Cooked egg noodles
- 2 Cups sour cream

Directions

1. Brown meat and onion in a skillet in the oil. Add the water, mustard and stir in tomato paste.
2. Add meat and the beef broth to the crock pot.
3. In the skillet, that you cooked the beef, add the butter and the mushrooms. Place into the slow cooker and combine well.
4. Cook for 7 to 8 hours.
5. Before serving, stir in sour cream and serve with egg noodles.

Hot Beef Sandwiches

Makes 8 sandwiches

Ingredients

- 1 Beef Rump Roast
- 1 tsp oregano Leaves
- 2 tsp sugar
- 2 Cups water
- 1 pkg. onion soup mix
- 1 Cup beef broth
- 3 cloves garlic, minced
- 16 buns

Directions

1. Cook the roast in a 4 quart slow cooker.
2. Ina bowl, combine all of the ingredients (minus the buns.)
3. Pour mixture over the roast.
4. Cover with lid and cook for 8 to 10 hours on low.
5. Slice the beef with a fork and place on buns.

Beef Tacos
Makes 8-12 servings
Ingredients

- 2 lbs. Beef Chuck Pot Roast
- 2 T. apple cider vinegar
- 4 tsp chili powder
- 12 corn tortillas
- 1 Cup sour cream
- 1 Avocado
- 4 Cups shredded lettuce
- jar salsa

Directions

1. Reserve 1 Cup salsa and add the rest of the salsa in the slow cooker.
2. Stir in the chili powder and the vinegar.
3. Add the beef to the crock pot and coat well.
4. Cook on low heat for 8-10 hours.
5. Using a fork shred the meat.
6. Add to a serving bowl.
7. Warm tortillas in microwave.
8. Top each taco with lettuce, beef, sour cream and avocado.

Beef Short Ribs

Ingredients

- 1/2 onion, chopped
- 5 pounds beef short ribs
- 1 jar barbecue sauce
- Salt
- Pepper
- 1 tsp vegetable oil

Directions:

1. Combine the onion and the barbeque sauce and add to the slow cooker.
2. Coat ribs with salt and pepper to taste.
3. Heat oil in a skillet on high heat.
4. Add ribs and brown on each side, coking for 4 to 5 minutes each side.
5. Add to the slow cooker.
6. Cook on low for 8 to 9 hours.

Slow Cooker Meatballs

Ingredients

1 slow cooker liner
 8 ounce jar sweet and sour sauce
2 T. soy sauce
1/2 Cup brown sugar
1/2 tsp black pepper
1/2 tsp garlic powder
3 pounds frozen meatballs
1 red bell pepper, chopped
1 can pineapple chunks

Directions

1. Place the liner in the slow cooker.
2. Add all of the ingredients to the pot.
3. Stir well.
4. Cook for 8 to 9 hours on low.

Beef Goulash

Serve 4 to 6.

Ingredients

2 lbs cubed beef stew meat
1 T. cooking oil
1 medium onion, diced
1 garlic clove, minced
1 tsp kosher salt
1/2 tsp coarse ground black pepper
2 tsp Hungarian paprika
1/4 tsp dried thyme
1 can (14.5 oz) diced tomatoes
1 Cup sour cream
3 green onions, chopped

Directions

Brown beef in oil with onion and garlic. Season with salt and pepper. Cook until browned on all sides. It doesn't have to be cooked through just browned. Add to slow cooker.
Add diced tomatoes, paprika and thyme. Stir to combine.
Cook on low for 6-8 hours.
Before serving stir in sour cream and green onions.

Beefy Meatball And Parmesan Soup

Serves 4.

Ingredients

1 lb ground beef
1 egg, beaten
1/4 Cup flour
1/2 tsp dried oregano
1/4 tsp garlic powder
1/2 tsp kosher salt
1/4 tsp black pepper
4 Cups beef broth
1 red bell pepper, diced
1 green bell pepper, diced
2 carrots, diced
1 small onion, diced
4 oz fresh Parmesan cheese, shaved into shards or coarse grated

Directions

1. Mix together beef, egg, flour, oregano, garlic powder, salt and pepper. Form into meatballs.
2. In slow cooker, add beef broth, diced peppers, diced carrots and onions.
3. Add meatballs gently to soup.
4. Cook on low 5-6 hours.
5. Add Parmesan cheese before serving.

Sloppy Joes

Ingredients

2 lbs. ground beef
1 large onion, chopped
3 carrots, chopped finely
2 celery stalks, chopped finely
1 green pepper, chopped finely
1 T. white vinegar
1 Cup ketchup
1 T. Worcestershire sauce
1 T. mustard

Directions

1. Brown beef and onion in skillet and drain off excess grease. Add to slow cooker.
2. If your kids don't like vegetable chunks, puree vegetables in blender. Otherwise finely chop vegetables with food chopper. Add vegetables to slow cooker.
3. Blend vinegar, ketchup, Worcestershire sauce and mustard together and pour over mixture in slow cooker. Stir to combine well.
4. Taste test and add more ketchup if you think it needs it.
5. Cook on high 5-6 hours.
6. Serve on hamburger buns.

This freezes well also so you could make extra for another day.

Slow Cooker Appetizer Recipes

Thai Chicken Wings - Crockpot
Makes 24 to 36 appetizers

Ingredients

3 lbs chicken wings
1/2 Cup salsa
2 T. peanut butter
1 T. lime juice
2 tsp soy sauce
2 tsp grated ginger

Directions

1. Add chicken wings to slow cooker.
2. Blend together salsa, peanut butter, lime juice, soy sauce and ginger.
3. Pour over chicken wings and stir to combine.
4. Cook on low for 4-6 hours.
5. Using a slotted spoon, take chicken out of slow cooker and leave the juices behind.
6. Place on serving platter.

Super Cheese Salsa Dip

Yields 5 cups dip

Ingredients

1 jar (16 oz) favorite salsa
4 Cups (16 oz) shredded American cheese
2 Cups (8 oz) shredded Monterrey Jack cheese
8 oz cream cheese, diced
1 Cup whole milk

Directions

1. Add salsa, cheeses and milk to slow cooker.
2. Stir to combine and cook on low for 4 hours.
3. Serve with fresh veggies and/or chicken strips.

Queso Dip

Makes 6 cups

Ingredients

1 onion, diced
2 tsp minced garlic
2 Cups diced tomatoes with jalapenos
1 can chopped green chilies
1 Cup milk
2 tsp Mexican seasoning
2 pounds white American cheese
Tortilla chips

Directions

1. In a bowl, sauté onion in a small skillet and in garlic. Add to slow cooker.
2. Mix in tomatoes.
3. Add cheese to the mixture. Stir until blended well.
4. Cook on low for 2 to 3 hours.
5. Stir before serving.
6. Serve with Tortilla chips

Pepperoni Pizza Dip

Ingredients

4 Cups cheddar cheese , shredded
1 T. minced onion
1 Cup mayo
4 Cups Mozzarella cheese
2 cans ripe olives
6 ounces mushrooms, sliced
1 package pepperoni slices, chopped
Crackers

Directions

- Use a 3-quart slow cooker for this dip works best.
- Add the olives, mayo, pepperoni, onion, cheese, mushroom in the slow cooker.
- Cook for 2 hours on low heat.
- Cover and cook another hour.
- Add remaining ingredients and cook 30 minutes.
- Serve with crackers and/or sliced vegetables.

BBQ Sausage Bites

Ingredients

- 1 package smoked sausages
- 1 lb. Bratwurst
- 1 pound Polish sausage
- 1 bottle barbecue sauce
- 1 cup orange marmalade
- 1/2 tsp ground mustard
- 1/2 tsp ground allspice
- 1 can pineapple chunks, drained

Directions

1. Combine sausages together in a 4-quart slow cooker.
2. In a bowl, combine marmalade, allspice and the barbecue sauce and mustard. Stir well.
3. Pour over the sausage mixture.
4. Cook for 3 hours on high.
5. Top with pineapples.

Slow Cooker Breakfast Recipes

Sausage & Egg Casserole
Serves 12

Ingredients

- 1 dozen eggs, beaten
- 14 slices of bread
- 2 1/2 Cups milk
- 3 Cups grated Monterey Jack cheese
- 1/2 tsp. salt
- 1 tsp. pepper
- 1 lb. sausage, cooked and drained or chopped ham

Directions

1. Grease slow cooker with butter or spray with cooking spray.
2. Layer the slices of bread in the crock pot. Add a layer of sausage, a layer of cheese,
3. Combine the milk, salt and pepper and the eggs in a bowl.
4. Add to the slow cooker.
5. Cover with a lid.
6. Simmer on low for 6 to 8 hours.

Maple Oatmeal

Makes 8 to 10 servings

Ingredients

- 2 Cups oats
- 4 Cups water
- 1/2 Cup dried apples
- 1/2 Cup maple syrup
- 1 Cup apple juice
- 1 tsp ground cinnamon
- 1/2 tsp salt
- 1/2 tsp Brown sugar
- frozen or fresh berries for topping

Directions

1. Combine the apples, apple juice, oats, maple syrup, water, cinnamon and the salt to a 4 quart slow cooker. Use a spoon to combine well.
2. Cover and cook on low 8 to 9 hours.
3. Place brown sugar and berries on top of the oatmeal when ready.

Slow Cooker Dessert Recipes

Slow Cooker Fudge

Makes 10 pieces of fudge

Ingredients

- 3 Cups dark or semi-sweet chocolate Chips
- 1/2 Cup canned coconut milk
- 1/3 Cup honey
- 1 tsp vanilla extract
- 1/8 tsp Sea salt

Directions

1. Put the chocolate chips, salt, honey and coconut milk in the slow cooker and stir well.
2. Cover and cook on low for 1 to 2 hours. Do not stir.
3. Turn the temperature on the cooker off.
4. Add in vanilla and combine well.
5. Allow mixture to cool for 5 hours.
6. Stir the mixture with a wooden spoon for 8 to 12 minutes.
7. Spray a cooking dish with non-stick cooking spray.
8. Put the fudge in the dish and cover.
9. Put in the fridge for 2 hours.
10. Cut into squares and serve.

5-Layer Crock Pot Brownie

Ingredients

- 1 package Brownie Mix
- 1/2 Cup melted butter
- 1/4 Cup water
- 1 egg
- 1/4 Cup coconut
- 1/4 Cup walnut
- 1/2 Cup oats
- 1 can sweet condensed milk

Directions

1. In a 2-quart mini slow cooker, combine the melted butter, brownie mix, egg, water and the milk. Stir until powder is dissolved and mixture is well combined.
2. Add half of the sweet condensed milk and a single layer of oats.
3. Add a layer of coconut and a layer of walnuts.
4. Cover the crock pot and cook for 4 hours on high.
5. Cut into squares to serve.

Bananas Foster

Makes 1/2 Cup

Ingredients

- 1 T. coconut oil, melted
- 1 T. fresh lemon juice
- 3 T. honey
- 1/2 tsp cinnamon
- 1/2 tsp vanilla extract
- 5 bananas, sliced

Directions

1. Combine the coconut oil, lemon juice, and honey to the slow cooker. Add bananas and coat well.
2. Cook on low for 2 hours.
3. Add vanilla to the slow cooker and stir to combine.

Slow Cooker Tips

To leave you with something extra, take a look at just a handful of easy cooking tips that will help make your slow cooker experience even more gratifying. Anyone can use these tips and benefits, but people new to the world of slow cooking will find them to be especially beneficial.

1.   Use fresh ingredients whenever possible. Fresh ingredients make an even better tasting meal.
2.   Ensure that your slow cooker is cleaned before you start. Also make sure that you take the time to wash your hands and to keep your work area sanitary as well.
3.   If you do not like one or more ingredients in a recipe, leave it out or make a substitute.
4.   Keep the lid on the pot once you turn it on. When you remove the lid you are not only taking away some of the great flavor you are also interfering with the way that the food will cook. Put it on and forget about it for a few hours.
5.   Always use a meat thermometer to check the internal temperatures of your meats. Sometimes it is hard to tell when a meat is done by simply looking at it, and we all know the dangers that lurk when you do not have the right temperatures on your cooked foods.
6.   If you want to make cleanup of the slow cooker a breeze, make sure that you add either nonstick cooking spray or parchment paper to the cooker before you begin. With the addition of either of these it is far easier to clean up.

7.   Always use the right size slow cooker. A pot that is too large can alter the cook times while a pot that is too small will not be able to prepare the dishes as they should be prepared. It is a good idea, if possible, to have a couple of crock pots available to handle your cooking needs at any time.

8.   Be sure that you pay attention to the amount that you are putting into the slow cooker, and always use caution so that you do not fill it too full. This can cause a big mess, not to mention ruin the entire meal and this is certainly not what you want to happen.

9.   Slow cooker meals are so easy to prepare it is easy to make your meals ahead of time. Many of the recipes in this guide can be frozen and prepared again. And, you can even prepare the menu for the week ahead, too. Make a shopping list with all of your ingredients and prepare ahead.

Slow cooker cooking is a way of life for many, and there are certainly benefits that can be found when you take on this new way of life, too. With these tips and these awesome recipes that is something that you can do like a pro. From this point forward you will never have to ask what's for dinner or look with dread when it is time to cook a meal for the family. These recipes are just that easy.   Now, let the goodness come alive and start using these recipes without delay!

13640782R00049

Printed in Great Britain
by Amazon.co.uk, Ltd.,
Marston Gate.